D1251111

339227

PRINTED IN U.S.A.

WILLIAM MORRIS
Wallpapers and Chintzes

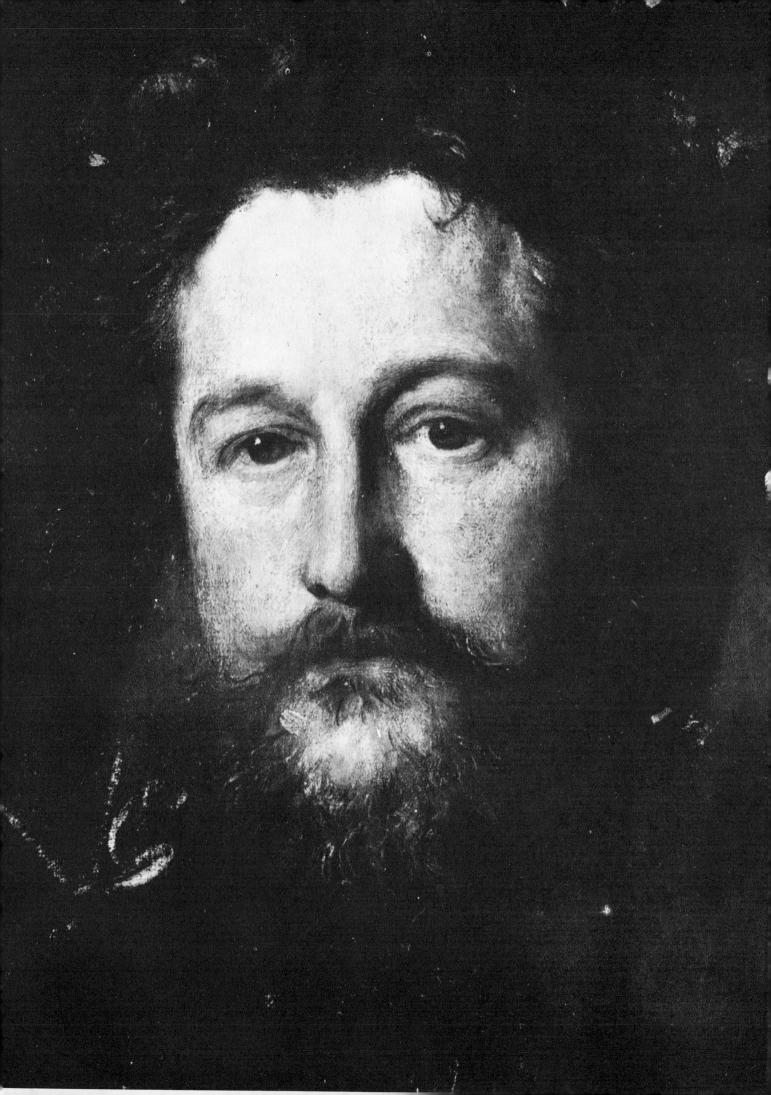

WILLIAM MORRIS
Wallpapers and Chintzes

Fiona Clark

With a biographical note by Andrew Melvin

St. Martin's Press • New York
Academy Editions • London

ACKNOWLEDGEMENTS

The author would like to thank the many people who helped her in her research especially the staff of the Whitworth Art Gallery, Manchester; the William Morris Gallery, Walthamstow; the Victoria and Albert Museum, particularly Mrs. Barbara Morris of the Circulation Department and Miss Linda Parry of the Textile Department and, Arthur Sanderson & Sons Ltd.

Frontispiece:
William Morris painted by George Frederick Watts, R.A. in 1880
National Portrait Gallery.

First published in Great Britain in 1973 by Academy Editions,
7 Holland Street, London, W. 8.

Copyright © Academy Editions 1973. All rights reserved.

Library of Congress Catalogue Number 73-89359

First published in the U.S.A. in 1973 by St. Martin's Press, Inc.,
175 Fifth Avenue, New York, N.Y. 10010.

Printed in Great Britain at the University Printing House, Cambridge
(Brooke Crutchley, University Printer)

Quarto
NK
1535
.M67
C55
1973

Contents

339227

Introduction

This book is intended as a "quarry" - a store of information for students within the field of William Morris's wallpaper and chintz patterns. The survey which follows lists and illustrates in chronological order all the designs which can be attributed to Morris. A "Guide to Sources" is included at the end, both to indicate the basis for the chronology and information given in the catalogue, and as a guide to further enquiry. It is hoped that in total this will provide a framework from which readers may make comparisons with the work of Morris's contemporaries and followers which are not attempted here.

Since Morris knew so clearly what he expected from his patterns, it may be helpful to preface this survey of them with a very brief account of these aims, as he expressed them in his lectures. Firstly, for Morris it was a measure of the crisis of art as he saw it that he should have to speak of "design" at all. For him, the tradition of popular art had been continuous from the earliest centuries until within two hundred years of his own time. Culminating in the art of the Gothic centuries and threatened by the stylistic degradations of the Renaissance, it had only truly declined with the technical innovations brought in by the eighteenth century and most fatally of all by his own. This tradition had rested on two things; firstly, on an equal society of craftsmen, undivided into employers and workers, and from the mid 1880s, Morris became involved, through the early Socialist movement, in an attempt to restore this. Secondly, it rested on the use of natural materials which necessitated the mastery of complex craft processes. In these conditions, "beauty" or "style" was an unconscious element which grew out of the struggle with process and as a result was inevitably suited to material and purpose. The best example of Morris "taking up the dropped links of tradition" is his revival of the dyeing techniques used throughout Western history and the perfection of the taxing indigo-discharge technique of printing cottons, a process which did in fact dictate its own particular colour scheme. However, the finality of this "break in the continuity of the golden chain" also brought hope of a new birth. Accordingly, from around 1879, from speaking in general terms of the problems of art, Morris began to give more practical advice on pattern design.

When lecturing on the history of repeating patterns, Morris always emphasized the crucial development as the discovery by the Gothic world of the "continuous growth of curved lines". This took two basic forms; "the branch formed on a diagonal line" and "the net formed on variously proportioned diamonds" - in fact the basic grids of Morris's own patterns. This type of complex, dynamic pattern suggested the richness and growth of nature itself, but could easily create an effect of restlessness, and Morris saw that the chief problem in organizing patterns lay in striking a balance between mystery and clarity. This was based on what he felt to be the needs of man in his "common workaday or restful times", when his imagination must be stimulated and refreshed but not overtaxed. One solution he adopted was to give his patterns a limited suggestion of depth, somewhere between a disturbing full relief and an unsatisfying flatness. This was achieved either by placing a major pattern over a subsidiary one; or by relieving tone on tone of the same colour (what he called a "damask" effect); or by bringing light colour out of dark. Similarly, he anchored the restless growing lines of his patterns firmly on the one hand to "the obvious presence of a geometrical order in the constructional lines of design" and on the other to "definite form bounded by clear outline" and "a Gothic crispness and clearness of detail".

Wallpapers and chintzes were "kindred arts", occupying the same lowly position in the hierarchy of crafts which for Morris was headed by painted decoration in the one field and tapestry in the other. This meant, however, that greater and not less care should be taken in designing patterns for these printed cloths and papers, which had no justification for their existence in the intrinsic beauty of their materials. Thus the guiding rules for pattern design outlined above applied both equally and especially to these two arts. However these differed in detail: with wallpapers for example, which lie flat, it was necessary to mask repeats more carefully; and on the whole Morris reserved his most formal patterns for chintzes designed to hang in folds. Furthermore, in wallpaper, the designer had to make conscious allowances for the nature of the materials, since the discipline of a difficult craft process was lacking. Accordingly, the designer had to impose his own limitations, and it was best "not to force the colour, but to be content with getting it either quite light or quite grey". Hence Morris's characteristic range of sage, rust, saxe blue. Chintzes offered "greater possibilities of rich colours from genuine dyes" and the limited range of vegetable dyes which Morris finally perfected at Merton Abbey gave their own characteristic harmonies, which he described as "frank reds and blues . . . the mainstays of the colour arrangement . . . softened by the paler shades of red, outlined with black and made more tender by the addition of yellow in small quantities, mostly forming part of brightish greens".

The final test of a pattern for Morris was its possession of "meaning". This is perhaps a surprising criterion for domestic papers and cottons, yet it is just this romantic conception of pattern which sets Morris apart from the rational arguments of his contemporaries. "You may be sure", he wrote, "that any decoration is futile . . . when it does not remind you of something beyond itself, of something of which it is but a visible symbol". This meant chiefly reference to nature, especially "those natural forms which are at once most familiar and most delightful to us, as well from association as from beauty". Morris's repertoire of motifs was in fact limited to the most traditional garden flowers (he spoke in his lectures against modern "cultivated" varieties and "exotics" of any kind); the birds in his Kelmscott garden and the wild flowers in the Thames Valley and of his Essex childhood. His observation of natural things was phenomenal and this is brought out in the closely-packed description of his garden in letters, especially to his daughter Jenny. Morris maintained however that flowers should be rendered with a degree of conventionalization in order to suggest to the viewer "not only the part of nature which to his mind . . . they represent, but of much which lies beyond that part." This suggestion of nature was further achieved by the growing and interlacing lines on which his patterns were formed.

However, it is also clear, though Morris does not say so, that reference to the tradition of Western art, and to its highest expression in the Middle Ages, was necessary to give meaning to a pattern. This emerges from his comments that though the Japanese were "admirable naturalists" their works remained mere wonderful toys, things quite outside the pale of the evolution of art". Morris's detailed knowledge of mediaeval textiles increased as he became more and more closely connected with the South Kensington Museum, now the Victoria and Albert; first as an examiner of student's work (1876); in the late 1880s as an adviser on the acquisition of historic textiles. The museum had a collection which was astonishly representative for this early stage of mediaeval studies, centred on the collection of the pioneer, Dr. Bock, whom Morris mentioned in several lectures.

Morris's patterns from 1876 onwards show that this historic knowledge brought increased formality and conventionalization, and was thus potentially at war with his naturalism, yet in his most characteristic designs he manages to reconcile them. Within a Gothic-derived net of incredible complexity, he combines from two to five different plants without destroying the natural system of growth peculiar to each. These patterns create a "bower" or "garden tangle" effect which was what he meant by representing Nature and not merely flowers. It is a synthesis which only Morris, with his sympathy for nature and his degree of identity with mediaeval art, could have achieved.

William Morris
a biographical note

William Morris's whole life was a paradox. For all his rude health, great strength and his hearty manners, he was nervous, excitable and died comparatively early. These contradictions were paralleled in other ways throughout his life. He preached and honestly believed in socialism and did what he could to alleviate the conditions of the working-classes. But he inherited a fortune from a Devonshire copper mine, an industry where some of the worst working conditions in England obtained. His success at producing expensive wallpapers and books caused him to admit that he was "as much a man of business as any of them"; and at the same time that he was an active revolutionary socialist, he was decorating Balmoral and St. James's Palace. As he once bitterly remarked "I spend my time ministering to the swinish luxury of the rich".

Morris was born in 1834, the son of prosperous middle-class parents. His father was a bill broker with a considerable fortune in mining shares which was to provide his son with a comfortable income for most of his life. When Morris was thirteen, he was sent to Marlborough. There he showed little interest in the usual subjects. Instead he devoted his time to medieval history, visiting local churches, taking brass rubbings and assimilating a wide knowledge of English Gothic architecture.

From Marlborough, he went to Exeter College, Oxford, possibly with the intention of going into the church. Certainly his mother had always understood that that would be his future career. It was at Oxford, however, that Morris met with people and ideas that were to completely change his life. Edward Jones (later to change his name to Burne-Jones) was his first and best friend at Oxford and he introduced Morris to William Faulkner who was to be a founder-partner of Morris's first firm. They were both to remain Morris's close friends throughout his life. It was also at Oxford that Morris first read the works of Ruskin; *The Seven Lamps of Architecture* and *Modern Painters* took on the importance almost of sacred texts and were to be the greatest single influence of Morris's life. All his beliefs on art, the importance of individual craftsmanship, and socialism can in essence be traced back to Ruskin. It was also through Ruskin that Morris first heard of the Pre-Raphaelites.

After leaving Oxford, Morris was articled to G.E. Street, the architect. He liked the work—his belief in the pre-eminence of architecture as a craft was to remain with him always—but he was unable to reconcile it with his growing interest in painting and his involvement with his Oxford friends, and new ones such as Dante Gabriel Rossetti, who were taking up an increasing share of his time. In addition to his competing interests in architecture and painting, Morris now also found time to write his first poetry and turn his attention to interior design. His career as an interior decorator began with the building and decoration of the Red House. at Upton, which was built for him and his wife by Philip Webb. The house was built to Morris's specifications, but when it was completed, he could not find any furnishings which he considered suitable. He was to write later, "I well remember when I was first setting up house some twenty-three years ago, what a rummage there used to be for anything tolerable in the way of hangings for instance".

The decoration of the Red House was thus entirely carried out by Morris and his circle. Its vaguely Gothic architecture was complemented by stained glass, woollen tapestry wall hangings and painted ceilings that took several years to complete. From this, his first exercise in interior decoration, Morris had the idea of extending the scope of his work and bringing his convictions to a wider public by the commercial production of suitable designs. In 1861, the firm of Morris, Marshall & Faulkner was founded.

The first prospectus of the firm castigates the state of decoration in England and then goes on to explain the advantages of Morris, Marshall & Faulkner whose "Artists having for so many years been deeply attached to the study of the Decorative Arts . . . have felt more than most people the want of some one place where they could either obtain or get produced work of a genuine and beautiful character. They have, therefore, now established themselves as a firm for the production, by themselves or under their supervision of murals, architectural carvings, stained glass, metal work and furniture."

Morris's most prolific period as a designer now began. In 1864, he had designed three wallpapers but in 1872 he started producing a steady stream of designs that was not to end until shortly before his death. Not even the break-up of the original firm and the foundation of Morris & Co., coupled with all the personal conflicts that this involved, could stop his prodigious output. In six years, Morris designed sixteen wallpapers and twenty-two fabrics. He also wrote an enormous amount of poetry, much of it based on the Norse legends he had heard during two visits to Iceland in 1872 and 1873. His poetry was, indeed, so well thought of that he was offered, but refused, the poetry chair at Oxford.

It is not easy to say when Morris first became interested in politics, but the seed of his interest in socialism was sown when he first read Ruskin's works. Morris's belief in the value and dignity of craftsmanship is closely related to the theory of the intrinsic value of work discussed in *Das Kapital*, which he read in 1883; but the inevitability of Morris's socialism can best be seen from his speeches and letters of the 1880's, in which he deplored the inability of the poor to appreciate art, simply because of their poverty. He wrote to the *Manchester Examiner* in 1883, "The absence of popular art from modern times is more disquieting and grievous to bear for this reason than for any other, that it betokens that fatal division of men into cultivated and degraded classes which competitive commerce has bred, and fosters; popular art has no chance of a healthy life or indeed of a life at all until we are on the way to fill up this terrible gulf between rich and poor". In the same year he joined the Democratic Federation. He was an active socialist for some years but in the end he lost interest, and besides he had also, by the late eighties, discovered a new interest which was to occupy fully the last few years of his life. This was the Kelmscott Press.

Morris's interest in printing grew fairly late in his life. He had made a few preliminary attempts to print his own poetry, but it was only in 1888, after the Arts and Crafts Exhibition of that year, that he started to produce his own books at the Kelmscott Press. Such was the success of the Press, that by 1897, although the equipment was little more advanced than that used by Caxton, sixty-three volumes had been produced there; all of them meticulously designed and—despite Morris's fears that commercialization would ruin the quality of the Press's work—all equally well produced. The influence of the Kelmscott Press was immense. Not only was it the forerunner of the private press movement, it also immeasurably raised the standard of typography in mass-produced books. Possibly the finest of all the books Morris produced there is the *Chaucer*. He died shortly afterwards on October 3rd , 1896, outlived by his delicate wife, who had been a semi-invalid for the whole of their married life.

Andrew Melvin 1971

Catalogue of Wallpapers

NOTES

See "Guide to Sources" for all authorities mentioned in the text.
DATES: The majority of the papers can be reliably dated from their entry either in the Patent Office Design Register or in the Jeffrey pattern books. They are illustrated as nearly as possibly in sequence as produced, except the ceiling papers, which are dealt with separately at the end.

PRINTING: Details of printing are not given in each case as all the papers were hand-printed by Jeffrey & Company in distemper colours from wood blocks.

SIZE: With one or two minor exceptions, Morris & Co. wallpapers were made in widths of 21 inches trimmed, 22 inches untrimmed. The size of the Repeat is noted in each case as this gives some idea of scale and of the shape of the pattern grids on which Morris worked. Dimensions are given: Height x Width.

MORRIS'S ORIGINAL DESIGNS: Where these are in Public Collections, this has been given as follows:-

Birmingham: City Museum and Art Gallery, Birmingham.

V. & A: Victoria and Albert Museum, London.

Walthamstow: The William Morris Gallery, Walthamstow.

Of the remainder, many were dispersed without trace after the sale of Morris & Company's effects in 1940, but are illustrated in two works written before that date:

Illustrated Lewis F. Day:

Lewis F. Day, "The Art of William Morris", *Easter Art Annual* 1889 (extra number of the *Art Journal*)

Illustrated Gerald H. Crow:

Gerald H. Crow, *William Morris Designer*, published by *The Studio*, 1934.

---

1. **DAISY** 1864
    Repeat: 14 inches x 10½ inches

    With the two papers which follow, this forms a group designed in 1862, within a year of the founding of Morris, Marshall, Faulkner and Co. Morris made an attempt to print them himself in the Firm's tiny premises at Red Lion Square, using etched zinc plates instead of wood blocks and transparent rather than distemper colours. In 1864, when the designs were handed over for printing by Jeffrey & Co., Metford Warner was already acting manager; as Managing Director he was to become the most respected figure in the wallpaper industry, and relieved Morris thereafter of any concern with production.

    Variants of this design were used for painting tiles and quarries (small stained glass panels) made in the early 1860s, and for embroideries at Red House.

2. **FRUIT** or **POMEGRANATE** 1864
    Repeat: 21 inches x 21 inches Original Design: Illustrated by Gerald H. Crow

    This pattern, and *Trellis* which follows, are based on an exactly square grid, with which Morris would be familiar from designing the painted tiles which were a staple product of the Firm in its earliest years.

3. **TRELLIS** 1864
   Repeat: 21 inches x 21 inches   Original Design: Walthamstow

The first of the group to be designed, this was probably based on the rose trellises which bordered the central quadrangle at Red House, Morris's home from 1860-65. In addition to the trellises, there were sunflowers, square-hedged garden plots and an orchard, the whole forming the first example of a type of garden - based apparently on Elizabethan and "traditional" cottage gardens - which Morris later advocated in his lectures, and which influenced architects of the Arts and Crafts movement.
The birds were designed by Philip Webb, architect of the Red House, who supplied all the animal life in the Firm's early stained glass.

4. **VENETIAN** c. 1868-70
   Repeat: 10½ inches x 22 inches

Morris's three initial designs had each required 12 blocks and had been relatively expensive to produce: the Venetian and five undated designs which follow in the Jeffrey records, are all monochrome papers adapted from historical designs. This change is partly attributable to the influence of Warington Taylor, energetic business manager of the Firm from 1865 to his death in 1870. In a letter of 1869 to Philip Webb, he points out the extravagance of producing more wallpaper designs than were likely to sell in view of the Firm's limited domestic commissions. It also emerges from this same letter that the designs were in fact submitted by architects closely connected with the Firm during this period, when it owed its survival largely to the goodwill of architects.

5. **INDIAN** c. 1868-70
   Repeat: 26½ inches x 22 inches

Taylor refers to this paper in the same letter of 1869 as "Scott's 'Indian.'" Scott has not been identified but is possibly George Gilbert, son of Sir Gilbert Scott and architect of Peterhouse College, Cambridge, where Morris and Co. were doing some decorative work from 1868-74. It is closely based on Indian designs for painted or embroidered furnishings.

6. **DIAPER** c. 1868-70
   Repeat: 5¼ inches x 5¼ inches

This design is adapted, not from historic examples, but from painted tiles designed by Morris in the late 60s and early 70s - see especially one of 1870 illustrated by Lewis F. Day.

7. **QUEEN ANNE** c. 1868-70
   Repeat: 12 inches x 22 inches

This must be the design referred to by Warington Taylor (see above letter) as "Townshend's 'Bird.'" Townshend is also known to have contributed *Spray* (see entry for this paper).

8. **SPRAY** c. 1871
   Repeat: 20 inches x 21 inches

From evidence provided by his daughter, it is known that the architect Charles C. Townshend sent Morris in 1866 a sample of an old wallpaper taken from a house in

Bandon, County Cork, which was the prototype for this paper. It has therefore been grouped with the adapted papers, although its entry in the Jeffrey records appears after *Scroll.*

9. **SCROLL** c. 1871
Repeat: 29 inches x 21 inches

This is the first of a series of fine naturalistic designs which mark the resumption of original designing by Morris. In 1870, he took up the art of illuminating books and produced four within the next two years. The delicate pointed leaves and easy free-flowing scrolls recall the hand-painted floral decoration of these books.

10. **BRANCH** c. 1871
Underprint of above

11. **LARKSPUR** 1872 (Polychrome version 1874)
Repeat: 14¾ inches x 21 inches

An informal meander design, throwing off scrolls or sprays to right and left is the characteristic pattern structure of the group naturalistic papers produced before 1876 (see also *Scroll, Jasmine, Marigold* and *Vine*).
The same design was used for a chintz in 1875.

12. **JASMINE** 1872
Repeat: 28 inches x 21 inches Original Design: Birmingham

Here the apparently random offshoots from the stem are used to give a suggestion of tangled growth.

13. **LILY** 1874
Repeat: 12 inches x 21 inches

A return to the simple "powdered" pattern of *Daisy:* that is, the leading lines are not followed continuously by the motifs used in the pattern, but are only traced out in the form of dots or "powderings".

14. **VINE** 1874
Repeat: 21 inches x 21 inches Original Design: Illustrated by Lewis F. Day

By grouping motifs of apparently the same type and size (here the bunches of grapes) without making them either mirror images or repeats, Morris tends to disguise the mechanical nature of his pattern. This is the furthest he ever went in this direction.

15. **POWDERED** 1874
Repeat: 10½ inches x 20½ inches
Later produced as a chintz.

16. **MARIGOLD** 1875
Repeat: 10½ inches x 10½ inches

This wallpaper was registered in 1875, but may possibly date from c. 1873, since it appears in the Jeffrey records between *Jasmine* and *Lily.* The design was registered as a chintz later in the same year.

17. **WILLOW** 1874
Repeat: 17½ inches x 21 inches

18. **ACANTHUS** 1875
Repeat: 26 inches x 21 inches Original Design: Birmingham and V. & A. (two versions)

By far the most ambitious design yet attempted, requiring thirty colour blocks. Coming after the naive early designs, this anticipates the ample, stately designs that Morris was to produce in the late 80s.

19. **PIMPERNEL** 1876
Repeat: 16½ inches x 21 inches Original Design: Illustrated by Lewis F. Day

This is the first example of Morris using a "turnover" pattern, derived from his experience of designing for woven textiles, beginning in this year, 1876 (see entry for *Honeysuckle* in catalogue of chintzes).
With *Acanthus* and the two papers which follow, this forms a group of papers with a greater effect of solidity than any others designed by Morris. He was later to abandon the tonal shading seen here in favour of lighter or more linear patterns.

20. **WREATH** 1876
Repeat: 19½ inches x 10½ inches

21. **(THE) ROSE** 1877
Repeat: 22 inches x 21 inches Original Design: Illustrated by Lewis F. Day

22. **CHRYSANTHEMUM** 1877
Repeat: 21 inches x 21 inches Original Design: Walthamstow

An elaborate and costly embossed, gilt and lacquered version of this design was also produced. This was used in the drawing room at 1, Holland Park, the home of Alexander Ionides, decorated by Morris & Co. and many other artists including Walter Crane and William de Morgan, and the most sumptuous of all Aesthetic interiors. However, gilt and lacquered papers were part of the regular production of the Firm, beginning with the issue of *Vine* in this form in 1876. They possibly reflect the current Aesthetic fashion for wallhangings of stamped and gilt Spanish leather, which may in itself derive from the panels of leather used on the Firm's earliest furniture.

23. **APPLE** 1877
Repeat: 12 inches x 10½ inches

A return to a simpler paper, incorporating only three blocks.

24. **BOWER** or **THE BOWER** 1877
Repeat: 21 inches x 21 inches

25. **SUNFLOWER** 1879
Repeat: 16 inches x 21 inches

With *Acorn* (below) this is the most rigid example of a vertical "turnover" pattern which Morris ever used for wallpaper. A gilt and lacquered version was also produced.

26. **ACORN** 1879
Repeat: 19 inches x 21 inches

Gilt and lacquered version also produced.

27. **POPPY** 1881
Repeat: 17¾ inches x 10½ inches

Also produced with a gold and silver outline print.

28. **ST. JAMES'S** 1881
Repeat: 47 inches x 44 inches   (2 widths needed to make up one repeat)   Original Design: Walthamstow

The only public commissions ever undertaken by the Firm were both carried out in 1866-67: the Armoury and Tapestry rooms at St. James's Palace and the Green Dining Room at The South Kensington Museum. The Royal commission seems at first sight the more unlikely for an obscure firm of art-decorators but the two are possibly connected through the influence of Richard Redgrave, who was both on the staff at South Kensington and, in his capacity as Surveyor of the Queen's pictures, was reorganizing the paintings at St. James's from 1864 onwards. Once secured, the commission was extended in 1881-2 to the entire re-decoration of all the State Rooms and approaches, involving carpets, painted decoration and two specially designed patterns, the *St. James's* silk damask and this wallpaper for the Throne Room and Wellington Room. Other Morris papers were used in the lesser rooms, including *Jasmine* and *Sunflower*. 68 blocks and 2 change blocks were needed to print the design.

29. **ST. JAMES'S CEILING** 1881
Designed for use with the above

30. **CHRISTCHURCH** 1883
Repeat: 10½ inches x 10½ inches

From around this date, there seems to be no dominant influence on the designs and the result is a rather bewildering variety of styles. This may be explained by Morris's absorption first in textile printing at Merton Abbey from 1882 and later (1883) in tapestries. However, he may have come to see this variety as a necessary condition of wallpaper manufacture. A Morris & Company brochure, issued for the Boston Foreign Fair in 1883 gives detailed advice on different styles of paper for different types of rooms.

31. **GRAFTON** 1883
Repeat: 10½ inches x 10½ inches Original Design: V. & A.

The only occasion on which Morris used a stencil effect.

32. **WILD TULIP** 1884
Repeat: 25½ inches x 10½ inches

In this and many of the following papers, Morris makes extensive use of dotting, both as a form of shading on leaves and as a background. These dots were produced by metal pins driven into the wooden block, and Morris came to consider this mechanical method more suited to the nature of wallpaper and textile printing than modelled shading (see entry for *Lea* 1885 in chintz catalogue).

33. **FRITILLARY** 1885
Repeat: 22½ inches x 10½ inches   Original Design: Illustrated by Lewis F. Day

This sees a much greater use of conventionalization in the treatment of flowers - note especially the regularized chequerboard markings on the fritillary.

34. **LILY AND POMEGRANATE** 1886
Repeat: 28½ inches x 20¾ inches Original Design: Walthamstow

35. **WILLOW BOUGHS** 1887
Repeat: 28½ inches x 10½ inches

Here Morris returns to the wayward growth of his earlier patterns, though the underlying structure is the same vertical meander with a subsidiary "broken" horizontal line which he used in more emphatic form in his contemporary chintz designs.

36. **BRUGES**   1888
Repeat: 24 inches x 21 inches

A rather sombre design, imitating the effect of a damask fabric. It was also produced in versions with a mica ground and a flock pattern.

37. **AUTUMN FLOWERS** 1888
Repeat: 33½ inches x 21 inches Original Design: Illustrated by Lewis F. Day

A flock version of this design was produced.

38. **NORWICH** 1889
Repeat: 34 inches x 21 inches Original Design: Illustrated by Lewis F. Day

A year previously, Morris had written in his essay "Textiles": "Do not be afraid of large patterns; if properly designed they are more restful to the eye than small ones: on the whole, a pattern where the structure is large and the details much broken up is the most useful".   A tendency towards larger patterns can be seen developing in Morris's designs from the early 80s.

39. **WALLFLOWER** 1890
Repeat: 14 inches x 10½ inches

40. **HAMMERSMITH** 1890
Repeat: 18 inches x 10½ inches

41. **PINK AND ROSE** 1890
Repeat: 32 inches x 21 inches   Original Design: Illustrated by Lewis F. Day

Another large-scale pattern, in which Morris combines naturalistic flowers and a conventional symbol derived ultimately from near-Eastern art.

42. **TRIPLE NET** 1891
Repeat: 26 inches x 21 inches

This kind of rigid two-dimensional pattern, with only a minimal use of flower motifs, was usually reserved by Morris for ceiling papers.

43. **FLORA** 1891
Repeat: 17½ inches x 21 inches

This design was issued, at approximately the same date, as *Trail* chintz.

44. **BACHELOR'S BUTTON** 1892
Repeat: 18½ inches x 21 inches   Small Sketch Design: Illustrated by Lewis F. Day

45. **BLACKTHORN** 1892
Repeat: 25 inches x 22 inches   Original Design: Illustrated by Gerald H. Crow.

This is perhaps the supreme example of Morris's ability to combine a number of different plant growths (here, five) within an exceptionally complex geometric structure (a net built up on a vertical "turnover" pattern). The flowers are treated with a degree of naturalism not used by Morris since the late 70s.

46. **LECHLADE** 1894
Repeat: 36½ inches x 22 inches

47. **SPRING THICKET** 1894
Repeat: 30 inches x 22 inches

A strongly marked net pattern very similar to *Lily and Pomegranate.*

48. **COMPTON** 1896
Repeat: 33 inches x 21 inches Small working drawing (from Morris & Co. workshops): Walthamstow

Commissioned by Laurence Hodson for his house, Compton Hall, near Wolverhampton. It shows a return to a much less structured pattern: flowers are scattered in the fillings between the meanders, rather than being closely woven in with the rest of the design. Also produced as a chintz of the same title.

49. **MYRTLE** 1899
Repeat: 33 inches x 21 inches

Morris and Company issued this paper after Morris's death in 1896, from a design of his for needlework c. 1875.

Ceiling Papers

Ceiling papers posed special problems of design: whereas with wallpapers Morris allowed a limited depth and the suggestion of movement and growth, in ceiling papers it was essential that design should be entirely two-dimensional and without directional lines. This was achieved by relieving darker tones or colours on a lighter ground, with a minimum of shading, and by arranging the pattern symmetrically about crossed axes.

Morris seems to have designed these ceiling papers reluctantly: in his lecture "Making the Best of It" (c. 1879) he admits he would have preferred one of the historical alternatives of rafters, fresco or moulded plaster, but suggests white paint as a compromise measure, since a room papered all over would be "like a box to live in".

50. **CEILING** 1877
    Repeat: 21 inches x 21 inches

51. **THE WREATH** 1884 (Not illustrated)
    Repeat: 21 inches x 21 inches

    Also known as *New Ceiling.*

52. **BORAGE** 1888
    Repeat: 21 inches x 21 inches

53. **NET CEILING** or **THE NET** 1895
    Repeat: 21 inches x 21 inches

(A fifth paper, *St. James's Ceiling* (1881) is illustrated with its matching wallpaper).

1.   Daisy

2.   Fruit or Pomegranate

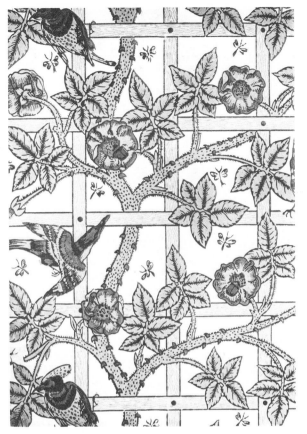

3. Trellis

4. Venetian

5. Indian

6. Diaper

21

7.   Queen Anne

8.   Spray

9.   Scroll *(detail)*

9. Scroll

11. Larkspur

10. Branch *(detail)*

12. Jasmine

13. Lily

14. Vine

15. Powdered

16. Marigold

17. Willow

18.　Acanthus

19. Pimpernel

20. Wreath

21 Rose

22. Crysanthemum *(detail)*

24. Bower

31

23. Apple

Cray ▶

◄ Daffodil

25. Sunflower

26. Acorn

27. Poppy

28. St. James's

29. St. James's Ceiling

31 Grafton

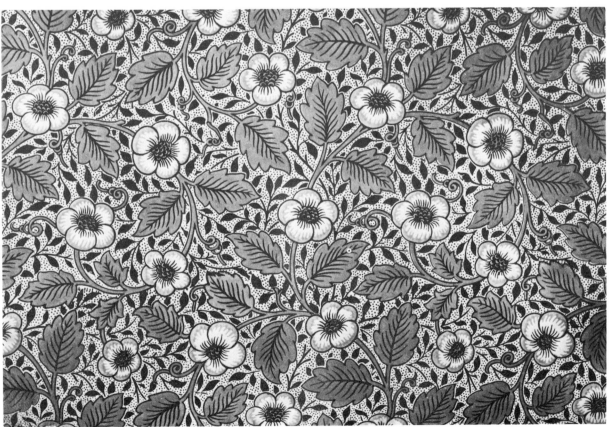

30. Christchurch

32. Wild Tulip

33. Fritillary

34. Lily and Pomegranate

35. Willow Boughs

36. Bruges

37.   Autumn Flowers

38. Norwich

39. Wallflower

40. Hammersmith

41. Pink and Rose

42. Triple net

44. Bachelor's Button

43. Flora

Trellis ▶

48

◄ Chrysanthemum

45. Blackthorn

46. Lechlade

47. Spring Thicket

47. Spring Thicket *(detail)*

48. Compton *(detail)*

48. Compton

49. Myrtle

50.   Ceiling

52.   Borage

53.   Net Ceiling

Borage chintz, block. Metal on a wooden base.
26.6 x 22.9 cm, 1883 (William Morris Gallery)

Catalogue of Chintzes

As for Notes to Catalogue of Wallpapers, with exception of:
SIZE: Morris & Co. chintzes were made in 36 inch widths (with the
exception of *Cherwell, Compton* and *Severn,* which were 27 inches).
PRINTING: As details of manufacture vary, the place where the design
was printed is given in each case.

CHINTZES: A NOTE ON DYEING AND PRINTING

The production of chintzes caused Morris more difficulty than any other of the decorative
arts he took up, and needs some explanation. The problem as he saw it lay not in the printing but in the colours themselves. Although machine-printing by rollers was well established
by the late 1860s, it was still possible to get hand-block printing done by better firms such
as Thomas Clarkson & Co., who printed chintzes for Morris from c. 1868. Morris's views
on dyestuffs were first expressed in his lectures of the 1880s, but were already behind his
dissatisfaction with Clarkson's and his alliance with Thomas Wardle in 1875. By his account,
the same vegetable and insect dyes had been used from the earliest times until the discovery of chemical dyes, beginning in the early nineteenth century, had eventually banished
them from commercial use in England. Morris wanted to re-discover these vegetable colours
for three reasons: firstly, he believed they were beautiful in themselves and harmonized
naturally with each other; secondly, they were not only permanent, but of equal permanence,
unlike the early chemical dyes, which faded quickly and unevenly, producing distortions
in design; and lastly because he hoped that the discipline of the old dyestuffs, with
their limited number of colours and difficulties of handling, would somehow combat the
futility of style which the easier methods had brought about. Between 1875 and 1878, he
carried out experiments with these vegetable dyes along the following lines: trial printings
of his designs were carried out by Thomas Wardle and two of his printers in a special division
of Wardle and Co.'s works at Leek, Morris keeping control over the work by letter and by
occasional visits to Leek. In addition, he carried out small-scale experiments at Queen
Square, following recipes in old herbals. At the beginning, very few of those trial printings
survived the tests - washing and exposing to light for a fortnight - carried out by Morris in
London, and he was always short of stock. By the end of 1876, in a letter to Wardle com-
plaining of the ineptitude of his printers, he had already concluded that no further progress
could be made without "constant artistic supervision on the spot". This was finally achieved
by the setting up of Morris & Co.'s own extensive printing works at Merton Abbey in 1881.

The most problematic of all the dyes was the blue dye, indigo, which was only soluble when
hydrogenated. At Leek, first Prussian blue and later a method of printing with indigo by
using chemicals to delay oxidisation had been used. Morris's achievement at Merton was to
revive the earliest method of using indigo, which was to dye the cloth totally and use a printed resist to produce the pattern (for a description of this process see entry for *Strawberry
Thief*). When he had fully mastered this "indigo-discharge" technique (around 1883) many
of the remaining chintzes printed at Merton were produced by combinations of the simpler
dyes: madder and kermes for red, weld for yellow and walnut and catechu for brown.

1. **JASMINE TRELLIS** c. 1868-70
   Repeat: 18 inches x 18 inches First printed: Thomas Clarkson & Co. at Bannister Hall, Preston

   According to May Morris, Clarkson's also printed some calendered chintzes from traditional designs for sale by the Firm (these may have been the same *Old English Chintz* designs which are listed in Morris & Co. catalogues of c. 1911). It seems likely that these were in fact adopted by the Firm as a compromise measure at a time when its domestic commissions were few - a parallel in type and date to the "adapted" wallpapers.
   Morris seems never to have abandoned a pattern, and even this naive early design was later printed by Wardle's.

2. **TULIP AND WILLOW** 1873
   Repeat: 16½ inches x 17½ inches First Printed: Thomas Clarkson & Co. Original Design: Birmingham

   Morris was not satisfied with Clarkson's printing of this design - it appears from his letters to Thomas Wardle in 1875 that the blue dye did not stand up to washing. However, it also emerges from this group of letters that Morris did not abandon Clarkson's altogether until late in 1876; that is until Wardle had managed to print cloth in any quantity.

3. **TULIP** 1875
   Repeat: 20½ inches x 8 inches Printed: Thomas Wardle at Leek Original Design: Walthamstow

   The first chintz design printed by Thomas Wardle for Morris.

4. **CARNATION** 1875
   Repeat: 9½ inches x 18 inches Printed: Thomas Wardle at Leek

5. **HONEYSUCKLE** 1876
   Repeat: 27 inches x 36 inches Printed: Thomas Wardle at Leek Original Design: Birmingham

   Morris wrote to Wardle that "Honeysuckle has cost us a lot in blocks, and is one of the most important we have or are likely to have". The pattern is certainly an ambitious one to have been attempted at a time when printing difficulties at Leek were so great: it achieves a density of growth unequalled by any of Morris's later designs. In this year, Morris made his first designs for woven fabrics, which were manufactured by various outside firms. He therefore took a keen practical interest in the mediaeval textiles in the South Kensington Museum, where he had just been given an official position as Examiner of student's work. The results of this study of woven textiles can already be seen in this design, where the pattern is so arranged that the motifs form exact mirror images on either side of a vertical axis. Known as a "turnover" pattern, this comes naturally from the techniques used in weaving, where it simplifies both the pointing and the setting up of the loom. In this early version, Morris attempts to mask the central axis or hinge of the pattern.

6. **INDIAN DIAPER** 1876
   Repeat: 4½ inches x 4½ inches Printed: Thomas Wardle at Leek

   Apart from his joint experiments in dyeing with Morris, Thomas Wardle (1831-1909) was concerned with reform in the textile industry in his own right. His own enthusiasm was for the development of "Tussore" or Indian wild silk as an alternative to the cultivated silk of declining quality used throughout Europe in the nineteenth century. Wardle was later to produce silk textiles at Leek from designs very similar to this one, closely based on traditional Indian patterns, and it is possible that this design of Morris's already reflects Wardle's knowledge of Indian art.

7. **AFRICAN MARIGOLD** 1876
Repeat: 22 inches x 36 inches   Printed: Thomas Wardle at Leek   Original Design: Walthamstow

Like *Pimpernel* wallpaper of the same year, this is an early, informal version of the vertical turnover structure, which Morris was to develop further as his knowledge of woven textiles increased.

8. **IRIS** 1876
Repeat: 19 inches x 13½ inches Printed: Thomas Wardle at Leek

In the autumn of this year, Morris wrote to Wardle ". . . our great difficulty with some of the patterns consists in the effect of them depending on a very nice balance of colour . . . in future I shall send you patterns which will less depend on nicety of shade". Although registered earlier in this year, this monochrome design with its mechanical dotted background seems to indicate that Morris was already modifying his designs in the light of printing difficulties encountered at Leek.

9. **BLUEBELL** 1876
Repeat: 18½ inches x 9 inches Printed: Thomas Wardle at Leek   Original Design: V. & A.
The framework of this design - interlacing lines forming nests of ogival patterns - is derived from a fifteenth century Rhenish printed linen in the collection of the South Kensington Museum.

10. **SNAKEHEAD** 1877
Repeat: 12½ inches x 9 inches   Printed: Thomas Wardle at Leek   Original Design: Birmingham

11. **POMEGRANATE** 1877
Repeat: 12¾ inches x 9 inches Printed: Thomas Wardle at Leek

12. **PEONY** 1877
Repeat: 6 inches x 6 inches Printed: Thomas Wardle at Leek
This design may possibly be by Kate Faulkner.

13. **LITTLE CHINTZ** 1877
Repeat: 4½ inches x 4½ inches Printed: Thomas Wardle at Leek
A small-scale version of the *Pomegranate* design.

14. **BROTHER RABBIT** 1882
Repeat: 17 inches x 8½ inches Printed: Merton Abbey Original Design: Illustrated by Lewis F. Day

By the end of 1881, Morris and Company had completed the move from Queen Square to the workshops at Merton Abbey. The new vats took some time to master, and the first chintzes produced relied on the simplest varieties of the method of indigo-discharge printing: here, the indigo-dyed cloth is printed with a bleaching reagent which reduced the design to a half-tone.

The structure of this design - an emphatic "turnover" pattern with small paired animals and birds - is based on the earliest models to have inspired Morris: Sicilian and North Italian woven silks of the thirteenth and fourteenth centuries, themselves based on Byzantine and earlier Eastern sources.

May Morris records that the Morris family were reading *Uncle Remus* at Kelmscott Manor around this date.

15. ROSE AND THISTLE 1882
Repeat: 23 inches x 9 inches Printed: Merton Abbey Original Design: V. & A.

This sees Morris combining naturalistic motifs - here, the delicately drawn rose and thistle - with conventions, mostly variations on the pomegranate, derived from mediaeval textiles. These conventions had already been used as the major theme of the design in *Snakehead* and *Pomegranate*.

16. BIRD AND ANEMONE 1882
Repeat: 20½ inches x 9 inches Printed: Merton Abbey

This design was issued at approximately the same time as a wallpaper and as a chintz. However, the type of repeat used, a narrow upright rectangle, suggests that it was conceived as a design for chintz. (As a general rule, the repeats of Morris's wallpaper patterns tend towards the square, as suited to a flat surface, while the chintz repeats form this narrow shape, suggesting the fold. This remains true even when Morris is adapting the narrow "turnover", the characteristic weaving structure, to wallpaper). The birds in Morris's earliest-designed wallpaper had been drawn by Philip Webb, but it seems that Morris later mastered the art of drawing them: he wrote in a letter to Wardle (1877) "I am studying birds now to see if I can't get some into my next design" (this was *Bird* woven wool, 1878).

17. WREATH NET 1882
Repeat: 4½ inches x 4½ inches Printed: Merton Abbey Original Design: V. & A.

With the next three designs, this forms a group of small-scale patterns unique in Morris's textile work. May Morris claims that these were intended principally as dress fabrics, and this was supported by the fact that the only occasion on which Morris spoke on the question of women's dress was in a lecture, "The Lesser Arts of Life", delivered in this year, 1882. They were perhaps intended to give practical support to the plea that women ". . . should insist on having materials for your dresses which are excellent of their kind . . . and that when you have a dress of even moderately costly material you won't be in a hurry to see the end of it". These fabrics were made in the same widths as the furnishing chintzes, and were probably also intended as curtain linings, in addition to the plain dyed cottons sold by the Firm for this purpose.

18. BORAGE 1883
Repeat: 4¾ inches x 4½ inches (also reduced version: 2 inches x 2 inches) Printed: Merton Abbey

A smock made in a yellow and white version of this design, worn by Morris and possibly made for him by his daughter May, is in the William Morris Gallery, Walthamstow.

19. **FLOWERPOT** 1883
Repeat: 4 inches x 4 inches   Printed: Merton Abbey

This seems to be the first of the indigo-discharge prints with the addition of colour blocks.

20. **EYEBRIGHT** 1883
Repeat: 5¾ inches x 4½ inches   Printed: Merton Abbey

21. **CORNCOCKLE** 1883
Repeat: 22¾ inches x 9 inches   Printed: Merton Abbey

An almost bizarre example of Morris combining familiar wildflowers with conventional symbols.   Here too, however, Morris was on sound historical ground: such juxta-positions (using figures or animals rather than flowers) can be found in Sicilian silks of the thirteenth century.

22. **STRAWBERRY THIEF** 1883
Repeat: 20 inches x 17½ inches   Printed: Merton Abbey   Original Design: Illustrated by Gerald H. Crow

This design, with its intricate structure and many colours, triumphantly marks the perfection of the indigo-discharge technique at Merton Abbey.   This technique was described in a Morris and Company catalogue of c. 1911: "The cloth is first dyed all over in an indigo vat to a uniform depth of blue, and is then printed with a bleaching reagent which either reduces or removes the colour as required by the design.   Mor-dants are next printed on the bleached parts and others where red is wanted and the whole length of material is then immersed in a madder vat calculated to give the proper tint.   This process is repeated for the yellow (welds), the three colours being super-imposed on each other to give green, purple or orange.   All loose colouring matter is then cleared away and the colours are set by passing the fabric through soap at almost boiling heat.
The final treatment in the process is to lay the cloth flat on the grass, with its printed face to the light, so that the whites in the design may be completely purified and all fugitive colour removed in nature's own way".

23. **WINDRUSH** 1883
Repeat: 22½ inches x 17½ inches   Printed: Merton Abbey

The first of a series of four designs which take their titles from the tributaries of the River Thames.   The Thames seems to have had a special significance for Morris - he liked to think that the same river which began in the upper reaches near his country home at Kelmscott Manor, Gloucestershire, flowed past his London house at Hammer-smith.   He named the latter Kelmscott House to emphasise the link between them. This introduces another historical convention used by Morris, what he called "the inhabited leaf",: the floral pattern within a symbolic flower or leaf, derived from near-Eastern art and the mediaeval textiles influenced by it.   See also *Evenlode* below.

24. **EVENLODE** 1883
Repeat: 21 inches x 9 inches   Original Design: V. & A.

The type of pattern seen here - a diagonal stem forming a continuous vertical line with offshoots making up a broken horizontal - comes from a fifteenth century Italian velvet which was acquired by the South Kensington Museum in this year, 1883. Like the other mediaeval pattern types which inspired Morris, it was introduced very tentatively (see *Windrush)* but developed into the bold insistent design of *Cray* and *Wandle.*

25. **KENNET** 1883
    Repeat: 25 inches x 9 inches Printed: Merton Abbey Original Design: Birmingham

Printed in monochrome and many-coloured indigo-discharge versions.

26. **WEY** 1883
    Repeat: 12 inches x 9 inches Printed: Merton Abbey Original Design: Birmingham

27. **ROSE** 1883
    Repeat: 20 inches x 17 inches Printed: Merton Abbey

It seems that for this design, Morris returned for inspiration to a sixteenth century Venetian silk and gold brocade which he had used three years earlier for his *Rose and Lily* woven silk. The bold ogival framework of the Venetian example can still be seen here, broken at the sides by foliage, and the crown which linked the ogees survives in vestigial form in the shapes of leaves.

28. **CRAY** c.1884
    Repeat: 36½ inches x 17½ inches Printed: Merton Abbey

This design produces the richest effect which could possibly be achieved on printed cotton.

29. **LODDON** 1884
    Repeat: 22 inches x 17½ inches Printed: Merton Abbey Original Design: Illustrated by Lewis F. Day

With the next eight titles, Morris extended his "river series" to major rivers.

30. **WANDLE** 1884
    Repeat: 36 inches x 17½ inches Printed: Merton Abbey Original Design: Illustrated by Lewis F. Day

Morris wrote to his eldest daughter Jenny in September 1883 that one of the chintzes he was designing was "Such a big one that if it succeeds I shall call it Wandle: the connection may not seem obvious to you, as the Wet Wandle is not big but small, but you see it will have to be very elaborate and splendid so I want it to honour our helpful stream". The Wandle was the stream which ran past the works at Merton and supplied water of the special purity needed for dyeing.

31. **LEA** 1885
    Repeat: 16½ inches x 18½ inches Printed: Merton Abbey

This design makes a very noticeable use of dots, both as background and shading, but the use of dots and hatchings can be seen in many of Morris's designs since its introduction in *Iris.* In his 1889 essay "Textiles", he notes that in printed cloths " . . . much use can be made of hatching and dotting, which are obviously suitable to the method of block printing" (Brass pins can easily be driven into a wooden block to print off as dots). Morris's use of dotting is an example of his belief that design should be the result of whatever processes were natural to the craft technique involved.

32. **MEDWAY** 1885
Repeat: 18 inches x 12 inches Printed: Merton Abbey Original Design: (for wallpaper) Birmingham (for chintz) Walthamstow

This design seems to have been issued as a wallpaper and as a chintz almost simultaneously: however, as its title links it with the river series, it has been included in this section. A much more open design than was usual with Morris and possibly influenced by Persian sources.

33. **AVON** c. 1886
Repeat: 32½ inches x 36 inches Printed: Merton Abbey Original Design: Walthamstow

This design also presumably belongs to the river series, and is by Morris in the absence of any evidence to the contrary.

34. **CHERWELL** 1887
Repeat: Printed: Merton Abbey Original Design: Walthamstow

With *Trent* and *Compton,* this marks a return to a more loosely organized design with the flowers placed apparently at random between the meander.
Issued around 1890 as a wallpaper with the title *Double Bough.*

35. **TRENT** 1889
Repeat: 34 inches x 36 inches Printed: Merton Abbey Original Design: Illustrated by Lewis F. Day

36. **YARE** c. 1890
Repeat: 14 inches x 14 inches Printed: Merton Abbey

This pattern and *Severn* c. 1890 (not illustrated) are by Morris in the absence of any evidence to the contary.

37. **DAFFODIL** c. 1891
Repeat: 14½ inches x 8 inches Printed: Merton Abbey Original Design: Walthamstow

This design was printed at Merton using chemical dyes, but it remained an isolated experiment as this was the last chintz designed by Morris.

1. Jasmine Trellis

3. Tulip

2.   Tulip and Willow

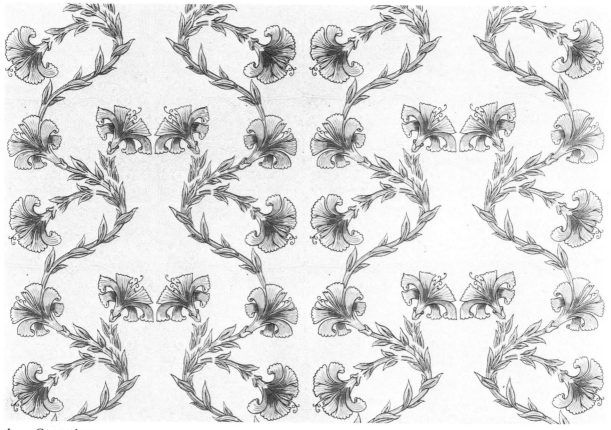

4. Carnation

5. Honeysuckle

Larkspur ▶

6.   Indian Diaper

◄ Willow

7.   African Marigold

8.   Iris

9.   Bluebell

10. Snakehead

11.   Pomegranate

13.   Little Chintz

12. Peony

14. Brother Rabbit

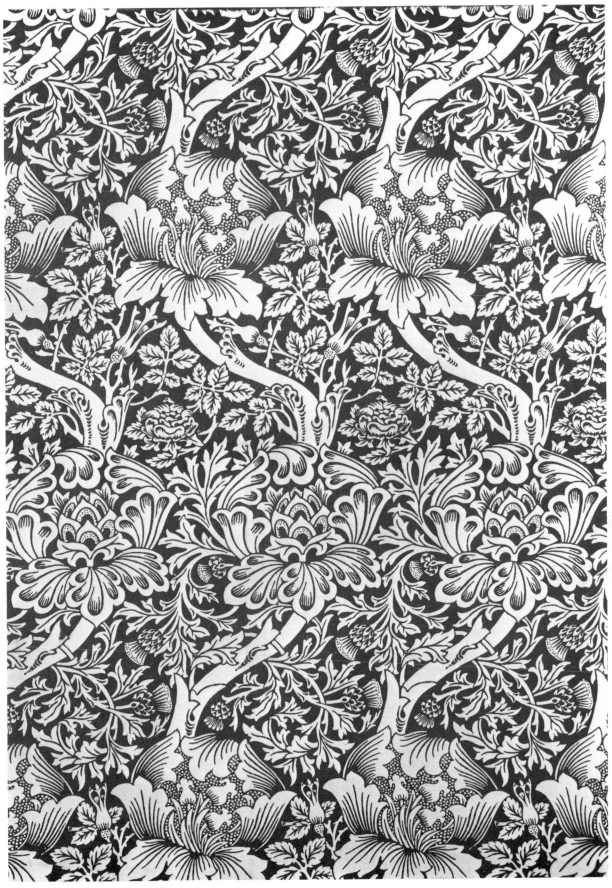

15. Rose and Thistle

16. Bird and Anemone

17. Wreath Net

18. Borage

73

19. Flowerpot

20. Eyebright

21. Corncockle

22. Strawberry Thief

23. Windrush

24. Evenlode

25. Kennet

26. Wey

Marigold ▶

◄ Bluebell

27. Rose

28. Cray

29. Loddon

30. Wandle

31. Lea

32. Medway

33. Avon

34. Cherwell

35. Trent

36. Yare

37. Daffodil

Sources

MANUSCRIPT SOURCES

General:

The Patent Office Design Register, Public Record Offices, London. The Copyright of Designs Acts, 1839 and 1840, extended copyright protection for the first time to designs in the decorative arts. They were an outcome of the same government concern for the low commercial and artistic standing of these arts in England which had earlier led to the setting up of the first Schools of Design (1836). From 1839 to around 1912, documented samples or photographs were kept of all designs so registered. Registration, being a method of self-protection for manufacturers, was purely voluntary - sixteen of the forty-nine wallpaper and twenty-six of the thirty-eight chintz designs noted earlier were in fact registered by Morris & Co. Nevertheless it is the largest and most reliable source for the dating of these designs.

Wallpapers:

Pattern Books of Messrs. Jeffrey & Co., Property of A. Sanderson and Sons Ltd. Jeffrey & Co. commissioned designs from nearly all the leading designers of the nineteenth century, but their Morris wallpapers were a special undertaking and were sold, not through the normal retail channels, but only from Morris & Company's showrooms. Accordingly, they kept two separate books of their Morris papers, with samples entered in order of production, noting date, price and number of blocks. Changes in all these details were recorded over a long period and some of the original entries have been obliterated. As a guide to dating it may be used to supplement the Register, though some of the samples may have been entered out of sequence. Although it has not been possible to list them in the survey of papers, these books provide evidence for all the original colourways, both those first printed and new colourings brought out during Morris's lifetime.

Chintzes:

Sixty letters from William Morris to Thomas Wardle on Dyeing and Printing 1875-77', Typescript in V. & A. Library.
Sample Books of Thomas Wardle and Co., Whitworth Art Gallery, Manchester.

These two sources are complementary. Thomas Wardle kept a record of all the trial printings made at Leek which he then sent to. London - Morris wrote back with detailed criticisms of them, quoting Wardle's sample numbers. Four books, 1875-79, cover the period of experimental dyeing and printing; a further five books, 1882-c. 1909, provide evidence that Wardle continued to print the designs he had pioneered with Morris even after the setting up of the Merton Abbey workshops in 1881. One book, dated 1891, contains samples of Morris patterns produced by roller-printing: contemporary with the printing of *Daffodil* at Merton in chemical colours, this may indicate either the extent of Morris's preoccupation with the Kelmscott Press or a change in his attitude towards modern means of production. The two remaining books in this collection illustrate Thomas Wardle's own textiles, including printed Tussore silk.

The Merton Abbey Dye Book:

A record kept by J. H. Dearle, Morris's assistant at Merton, of the dye recipes and printing procedure used for each design. This is privately owned, but two facsimile pages, displayed in the Textile study rooms at the V. & A., give an idea of the complexity of the old processes revived by Morris.

MORRIS'S OWN WRITINGS:

All Morris's major writings were published in a collected edition from 1910-14. Volume 12 of this, *Hopes and Fears for Art; Lectures on Art and Industry,* Longmans Green & Co., 1914, is devoted to his lectures on art. The earliest of these lectures, beginning with "The Lesser Arts" in 1877, are general diagnoses of the sickness of art;"Making the Best of It" (c. 1879) is transitional among these and does include some detailed ideas on pattern designing. The lectures which develop these fully are: "Some Hints on Pattern Designing", 1881 (A series of 18 large watercolour drawings of historical patterns and pattern grids, used by Morris to illustrate this lecture given at the Working Men's College is in the William Morris Gallery); "The History of Pattern Designing", 1882; "The Lesser Arts of Life", 1882; "Textile Fabrics", 1884.
Morris's occasional writings on art are reprinted in May Morris's *William Morris: Artist, Writer, Socialist* Volume 1, Basil Blackwell, Oxford, 1936. See especially two essays written as introductions to catalogues of the Arts and Crafts Exhibition Society: "On the Art of Dyeing", 1888, which gives in detail the history and properties of all the vegetable dyes revived by Morris, and "Textiles", 1889.

BIBLIOGRAPHY OF WALLPAPERS AND CHINTZES

For a full bibliography of Morris see section in William E. Fredeman, *Pre-Raphaelitism: A Bibliocritical Study,* Harvard, 1965. The three most recent books on Morris, all published in 1967 after this survey, each give a good picture of the whole range of Morris's activities and contain bibliographies: Paul Thompson, *The Work of William Morris,* Heinemann; Ray Watkinson, *William Morris as a Designer,* Studio Vista; Philip Henderson, *William Morris: His Life, Work and Friends,* Thames and Hudson.

General:

Peter Floud, "Dating Morris Patterns", *The Architectural Review.* Contains the result of the first detailed research made into Morris's designs after the retrospective studies by members of the Morris circle. Illustrates the mediaeval silks in the collection of the South Kensington Museum which Floud discovered and related to Morris's work.
May Morris, *William Morris: Artist, Writer, Socialist* Volume 1 (see "Morris's Own Writings"). The chapter "Morris as a Designer" contains a detailed account of the designs for printed patterns, inaccurate as to dating but a sensitive appreciation by one who herself designed wallpapers for the Firm.

Wallpaper:

Peter Floud, "The Wallpaper Designs of William Morris", *The Penrose Annual* No. 54, 1960. *Historic Wallpapers in the Whitworth Art Gallery,* Whitworth Art Gallery, 1972, provides a good background history of wallpapers and includes the Morris patterns.

Chintz:

Catalogue of an Exhibition of English Chintz: Two Centuries of Changing Taste (Assembled

by the V. & A. at the Cotton Board Colour, Design and Style Centre Manchester)H.M.S.O., 1955.
Again an excellent background history, including the Morris episode. Gives details of two "imitation Morris" chintzes produced by manufacturers in the late 70s and early 80s, evidence of his contemporary popularity.

PUBLIC COLLECTIONS WITH IMPORTANT HOLDINGS OF MORRIS WALLPAPERS AND CHINTZES

The following all have a complete or near complete range of patterns:

Victoria and Albert Museum, South Kensington, London:

The Print Room has a set of wallpapers kept by Morris and Morris & Co. pattern books; also the original designs noted in the text. Additional wallpapers are kept in the Circulation Department. The collection of chintzes is distributed between the Textile and Circulation Departments.

The William Morris Gallery, Lloyd Park, Walthamstow:

This museum's publication, *Catalogue of the Morris Collection,* includes all its holdings of wallpapers and chintzes up to the date of publication (1969). There is a small specialist library of books on Morris which serves also as a study room for students. A modern reproduction of *Bachelor's Button* has been used to decorate an exhibition room displaying Morris & Company furniture.

The Whitworth Art Gallery, Whitworth Park, Manchester:

A feature of this collection is several long (6 to 8 foot) lengths of chintzes of the Merton Abbey period, on loan from Manchester College of Art.

COMPLETE INTERIORS INCORPORATING MORRIS PAPERS AND CHINTZES

These are of three main kinds:

1. Decorative Schemes undertaken by Morris & Company. These were chiefly in houses built or altered by Philip Webb and were planned by Webb and Morris together. These domestic commissions were the most vulnerable aspect of Morris's work and none of the major ones have in fact survived. Some are, however, recorded in articles written shortly after Morris's death:
1, Palace Green (1868-81) *The Studio,* October, 1898
1, Holland Park (1876) *The Studio,* November, 1897
Buller's Wood *The Studio,* April, 1898
"Clouds", East Knoyle (1881-6) *Country Life,* November 15, 1904
"Standen", East Grinstead (1891) *Country Life,* May 7, 1910.
(This last survives but is not open to the public).

Of Morris's two public commissions, only St. James's Palace (1866-82) makes use of wallpapers. For a description of the original scheme and what remains of it see Charles Mitchell, "William Morris at St. James's Palace", *The Architectural Review,* January, 1947.

2. The second type of "Morris" interior - in which the owners ordered papers and chintzes,

from Morris and Co. without employing them to plan the decorative scheme - has survived rather better. The best example which is also open to the public is Wightwick Manor, near Wolverhampton, Staffs. (The National Trust). Many of the papers and chintzes which were hung on the walls when the house was built in 1887 are still in position; and the original contents have been added to in the form of portraits and mementoes of the Pre-Raphaelite circle so that the whole goes some way towards recreating the lost interiors mentioned above.

3.   Morris's Own Houses: Kelmscott Manor, near Lechlade, Glous. (Society of Antiquaries of London). May Morris came to live here permanently after her father's death, taking with her most of the contents of his London home, Kelmscott House. It fell into decay after her death in 1936, but has recently been entirely renovated and decorated throughout with modern reproductions of Morris papers and chintzes. Open to the public on several days throughout the year.

Finally, to discover how Morris thought his patterns should be used in room design:

His Lecture "Making the Best of It" (c. 1879, mentioned earlier) treats in detail every aspect of interiors and includes Morris's views on gardens.

A pamphlet, issued in conjunction with Morris & Co.'s exhibit at the Boston Foreign Fair in 1883, suggests ways in which the papers and chintzes should be used. It is quoted at length in Ray Watkinson's *William Morris as a Designer* (see Bibliography).

AFTER MORRIS & COMPANY

William Morris wallpapers and chintzes have been in production almost continuously for over one hundred years. Jeffrey & Co. carried on printing the papers until their closure in 1930, when the work was transferred to A. Sanderson and Sons Ltd. In 1940, when Morris and Co. went into voluntary liquidation, Sanderson purchased all the wallpaper blocks. Around 1950, they began to print a number of designs, using the original method of hand-blocking and they have issued a changing range of designs in successive collections ever since.

All the chintzes, including the ones taken over from Wardle's, c.1909, were printed at Merton Abbey until 1940. Stead McAlpin & Co. of Carlisle, purchased the blocks, and concessions to print from these were given first to The Old Beach Linen Co. and later (1959) to Warner and Sons. In 1965 Sanderson launched the first of their fabric collections, mainly using designs intended for wallpaper. The indigo-discharge method, however, ended with Merton Abbey: the early revived chintzes were direct surface printed and more modern ones are screen-printed.

Morris designs never suffered from the general reversion against Victorian art in the early part of this century, but there are signs that they are only now reaching the full height of their popularity. The John Lewis group of stores, affiliated to Stead McAlpin, currently produce a wide range of the fabric designs in modern colourings. In 1972, Coloroll entered the field with a collection of wallpapers from printed chintz designs. Aside from the revived designs, the standard current ranges reflect the influence of Morris as strongly as at the height of his contemporary popularity in the 1880s.

Chronology

1834 - William Morris born, 24th March, at Elm House, Walthamstow.

1848-51 - Educated at Marlborough College, Wilts.

1853-5 - At Exeter College, Oxford, to study for Holy Orders. Meets Edward Burne-Jones and C. J. Faulkner, later to be members of the Firm.

1856 - Articled to G. E. Street, Gothic Revival Architect, at Oxford. Philip Webb fellow pupil. Later in same year, moved to London to study painting under D. G. Rossetti.

1858 - First volume of poems, *The Defence of Guenevere,* published.

1859 - Marries Jane Burden.

1860-5 - Lives at Red House, Bexley Heath, Kent, specially designed for him by Philip Webb and decorated and furnished by Morris, Burne-Jones, Rossetti etc.

1861 - Firm of Morris, Marshall, Faulkner & Co. founded, with premises at 8, Red Lion Square, Bloomsbury. Daughter Jenny born.

1862 - May Morris born. Firm shows work at the International Exhibition in South Kensington.

1865 - Firm's premises move to 26, Queen Square, Bloomsbury with Morris and family "living above his shop". Warington Taylor appointed business manager.

1866-7 - Firm commissioned to decorate Armoury and Tapestry Rooms at St. James's Palace and Green Dining Room at South Kensington Museum.

1868 - *Earthly Paradise* published.

1871 - Rents Kelmscott Manor, Lechlade, Gloucs. First visit to Iceland.

1872 - Morris family go to live at Horrington House, Turnham Green, to make room for expansion of workshops at Queen Square.

1875 - Morris, Marshall, Faulkner & Co. dissolved and begun again as Morris & Co., with Morris as sole manager. First visit to Thomas Wardle at Leek.

1876 - Morris appointed Examiner (of drawings sent for competition) at South Kensington Museum.

1877 - Gives first lecture "The Decorative Arts". New sales and showrooms opened at 449, Oxford Street. Founds Society for Protection of Ancient Buildings. First woven silks produced at Queen Square.

1878 - Kelmscott House, Hammersmith taken. First "Hammersmith" hand-tufted carpets made there.

1881 - Morris & Co. moves works to Merton Abbey, Surrey.

1883 - High-warp tapestry weaving started at Merton. Morris's first involvement with Socialism - joins Social Democratic Federation.

1884 - Begins lecturing in London and throughout country on Socialism.

1885 - Leaves Social Democratic Federation and founds the Socialist League.

1890 - Leaves Socialist League and founds Hammersmith Socialist Society.

1891 - Kelmscott Press started. *News from Nowhere* published.

1896 - Kelmscott *Chaucer* published. Morris dies October 3rd, at Kelmscott House, Hammersmith.